WALKING IN BRITAIN

Scotland

Atholl Innes and Cameron McNeish

NEW
ORCHARD

CONTENTS

First published in the UK 1991 by New Orchard Editions
Villiers House, 41/47 Strand, London WC2N 5JE

ISBN 1-85079-168-6

Line drawings by Dudley Evans and William Lees
Cartography by Ron Rigby
Photography by John Heseltine

Printed in Great Britain by Biddles Ltd., Guildford and Kings Lynn

INTRODUCTION

Walking is a pleasure in itself, but it becomes doubly appealing if the route has the objective of visiting a place of special interest. All the walks in this series combine an interesting route with a visit to a well-known feature such as a beauty spot, caves, castle or museum.

The introduction to each walk provides a description of the walk's objective. Most are non-seasonal, and involve little additional walking in themselves once you are there.

Following the description of the objective, each section of the walk is clearly described, and a specially drawn map makes route-finding straightforward. As well as detailing the route, the authors describe many subsidiary points of interest encountered along the way.

The walks are varied and easy to follow. None of them is too taxing, except in the severest weather. Most are circular, returning you to your car at the starting point. Family walkers with young children will find plenty of shorter routes to suit their particular needs, whilst those with longer legs can select from more substantial walks.

The routes have been carefully chosen to include only well-established routes, and readers will certainly increase the enjoyment which they and others derive from the countryside if they respect it by following the Country Code.

Walk 1
THE QUIRAING, ISLE OF SKYE
HIGHLAND
2 miles

Skye has never had a great reputation amongst walkers, possibly because of its reputation as a Mecca for rock climbers and scramblers. Without any shadow of doubt the rocky spires and pinnacles of the Black Cuillin offer some of the finest mountaineering terrain in the country, but it would be a terrible injustice to ignore the Isle of Skye from the walker's point of view.

The Trotternish Peninsula that stretches northwards from the island's capital town, Portree, offers some fine walking terrain. For almost the full length of the peninsula runs the great feature of Trotternish, a long winding escarpment of basalt cliffs, running in a southerly direction from the steep peaks of Sgurr Mhor and Sron Vourlinn near Duntulm to the bare moorland above Portree.

The sheer east-facing cliffs of this great ridge are sills, or sheets of lava, immensely thick, intruded between the upper and lower layers of the basalt plateaux, after they were laid down. The upper basalt sheets have been cut back to the ridge, and have left the long intrusive sills in a long line from Portree, up the length of the peninsula, and out to sea as far north as the Shiant Isles.

While the east-facing cliffs are sheer, the western slopes of the ridge are in complete contrast. Long gentle grassy slopes run all the way to the rim of the cliffs, the turf shorn short and smooth by the continual grazing of sheep and rabbits and by the constant caress and occasional batterings of the westerly breezes.

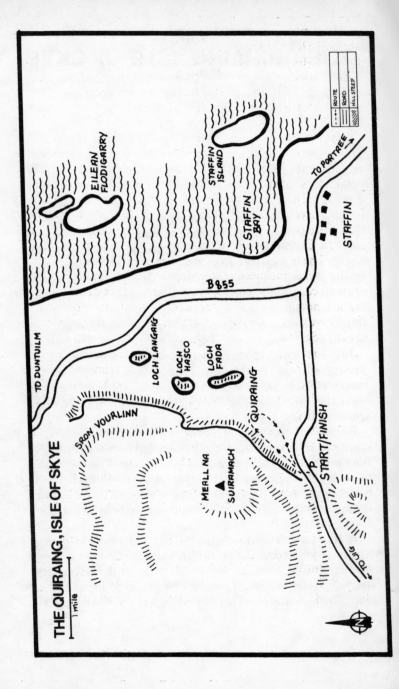

THE QUIRAING, ISLE OF SKYE

1 mile

EILEAN FLODIGARRY

STAFFIN ISLAND

STAFFIN BAY

TO PORTREE

STAFFIN

B855

TO DUNTULM

LOCH LANGAIG

LOCH HASCO

LOCH FADA

QUIRAING

SRON VOURLINN

MEALL NA SUIRAMACH

START/FINISH

P

TO UIG

N

ROUTE
ROAD
HILL STEEP

The summits of the ridge are not high, reaching 2,358 feet above sea level at the trig point on the Storr, but on a clear day these lowly hills offer superb panoramas as far west as St Kilda, beyond the Outer Hebrides, over the jagged outline of Skye's chief attraction, the Cuillin, to the great mountain masses of Torridon, Gareloch and Applecross on the mainland.

Close to the northern end of the peninsula, the cliff is broken up into a strange amphitheatre of spires, rocks and volcanic debris which has split away from the rock face of the basalt cliffs. Sited below the summit of Meall na Suiramach, this is the Quiraing, meaning a fold or pen. Only in volcanic Iceland have I ever seen formations like those in the Quiraing; contorted, bent, and strangely malevolent, like crooked fingers of rock beckoning you towards some other world. The mystic quality of the place is further emphasized by the lavish lushness of the slopes. Wild flowers grow in abundance, and the grass is an intense shade of green which has a tendency to soften the harshness of the landscape, almost creating a surrealistic effect. There is nowhere else like it in Scotland. It is unique and more than worth a visit.

Just south of the Quiraing, the long escarpment of the Trotternish ridge is breached by a road which runs across the backbone of the peninsula from Staffin to Uig. At the summit of the road there is a car park and this is where the track to the Quiraing begins.

Cross the road to the track and follow it eastwards as it rises gradually across the hillside, offering some fine views down towards Staffin and over the peat bogs to the sea and the mainland of Scotland. This track is a remarkably beautiful one with the wide sweep of the shore paralleling the sweeping fringe of the ridge which rises tier upon tier to a height of over 2,000 feet.

The first indication of the Quiraing is the Prison, the folds' southerly outpost, a massive assemblage of rock like some vast ancient fortress. No-one seems to know how this rock came by its name, but it is said that the ghost of some old cleric used to emerge from the rock from time to time, until

9

The Quiraing, a volcanic landscape freak of nature.

eventually he was put to rest by some good and kindly person.

Long dark corridors now take you away from the open slope and up past the towering spire of the Needle, 120 feet in height and tapering both at the top and the bottom. Above you immense crags, blocks and screes loom high, the slope leading upwards into the giant amphitheatre. Great slices of rock, fissured, weathered and cracked, stand apart from the main cliff behind, and through these great fissures you can gaze out to the contrasting pastoral scene below – the tiny crofts shrunk into insignificance, the green fields rolling and soft, and the swell of the sea breaking its surf on the great curve of Staffin Bay.

But another surprise awaits you. In this world of Titan verticalities, of grey and black upthrusts, it seems almost unreal to come across a high rounded table of lush cropped grass, as flat and smooth as a bowling green. This is the Table, the jewel of the Quiraing. A slanting ledge runs onto the surface of this wide upthrust, and behind it, perhaps in sympathy with the lushness of the unexpected turf, the riven

10

cliff face is a veritable rock garden. Yellow globe flowers, red and white campions, blue butterwort and sprays of golden roseroot offer a splash of colour to the shining black rock; the Hanging Gardens of Babylon couldn't have been finer. This could well have been the setting for Tolkien's Rivendell, home of Elrond and his Elvin folk, a magical place on a magical island.

You can return to the road by either the same path as you came up, or else drop down one of the steepish scree corridors eastwards, where another track circumnavigates the Quiraing. Once clear of the cliffs the path can be followed southwards then westwards and back to the Staffin-Uig road.

Walk 2
SANDWOOD BAY
HIGHLAND
4½ miles

If you're one of those people who can sit for hours
entranced by the continuous motion of pounding waves, then
Sandwood Bay is a marvellous place to visit. Of course, those
ancient Celts who lived by the sea had their lives dominated
by the pulse of the tides, and many now believe that the
moon, the co-ordinator of the tides, held a special signifi-
cance for these sea-going people.

One finds it easy to comprehend all this in Sandwood Bay
as great Atlantic rollers surge continuously into two miles of
gently curving bay fringed by whiter than white sands, sands
that are in turn fringed by these impetuous tides breaking
eagerly from pale green swell into white foam. Bisecting the
sands runs a long line of marram grass dunes; behind lies a
vast acreage of white sand, like some far-flung desert.

Away at the southern end of the bay a solitary sea-stack
rises from the water to guard the place. Called Am
Buachaille, or the Shepherd, it is a tall tower of Torridonian
sandstone which is a skyscraper of fulmar petrels.

Behind the bay the large freshwater Sandwood Loch holds
back the bleakness of the Sutherland moors, and gives the
whole place a depth of feeling that is lacking in most coastal
areas. To the north green headlands roll down to the sea
before tumbling into the Atlantic in precipitous cliffs, and
beyond the farthest of them the white tower of the Cape
Wrath lighthouse, the most north-westerly point of the
British mainland, lifts its head above the curving land.

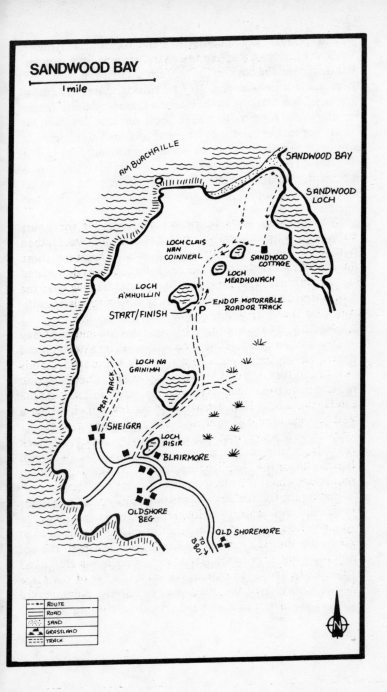

SANDWOOD BAY

1 mile

AM BUACHAILLE

SANDWOOD BAY

SANDWOOD LOCH

LOCH CLAIS NAN COINNEAL

SANDWOOD COTTAGE

LOCH MEADHONACH

LOCH A'MHUILLIN

END OF MOTORABLE ROAD OR TRACK

START/FINISH

P

LOCH NA GAINIMH

PEAT TRACK

SHEIGRA

LOCH AISIR

BLAIRMORE

OLDSHORE BEG

OLD SHOREMORE

TO B801

ROUTE
ROAD
SAND
GRASSLAND
TRACK

N

Sandwood Bay is singularly aloof and very lonely. Atmospherically the place is splendid and it's perhaps little wonder that this, of all the bays on the western seaboard, is supposed to be the hauling-up place for mermaids. Sandy Gunn, a shepherd, was walking in the marram grass sand dunes when his dog came running to him in some distress. Inquisitive, Sandy approached the spot where his dog had come from, a long spur of rock running out to sea near the southern end of the bay. There, at the seaward end of the spur, was a mermaid, sunning herself on a ledge. When the mermaid looked up and appeared to gaze in his direction, Sandy, now terrified, withdrew.

Trapped between the crashing breakers of the Atlantic and the rolling wilderness of the Sutherland moors, Sandwood Bay seems to infiltrate the spirit with a feeling of intense isolation – a feeling that to some people can be almost overpowering. There is, I am convinced, a fusion of one's own spirit and the very essence of that isolation, so that when you leave the place it's as though you are leaving a part of your soul there behind you.

Sandwood Bay is reached from the tiny hamlet of Oldshore Beg, some three miles north-west of Kinlochbervie in Sutherland. A peat road leaves the motor road between Blairmore and Sheigra, and a sign on the gate indicates that you can drive your car as far as Loch a'Mhuillin, saving, if you like, two miles walk in either direction. The peat road runs flat past the lochs of Loch Aisir and Loch na Gainimh, to Loch a'Mhuillin, where there is a good turning area. The rest of the route to the bay follows a good track across the rolling moors.

The walk across these moors isn't terribly exciting, but go on an early summer's evening and you will be accompanied by the 'drumming' of snipe and the 'birling' of golden plover, both birds of the wide open moors. Follow the track for two miles past Loch Meadhonach and Loch Clais nan Coinneal. Just after this second loch the path splits in two, the left-hand route taking you downhill into the bay, and the other leading to the ruin of Sandwood Cottage.

14

Mermaids and ghosts frequent Sandwood Bay amid the crashing Atlantic and the sound of gulls.

Follow the track down to the bay and enjoy the atmosphere of it in the company of fulmar petrels, kittiwakes, razorbills, seals and – if you're lucky, as I was – otters.

Return to your car by crossing the great area of sand immediately behind the marram grass dunes and skirt the northern edges of Sandwood Loch. On the hill above the loch you'll see the red roofed Sandwood Cottage, used nowadays as a walkers' shelter. This is well worth a visit because there is a strange story attached to it. It relates to an Edinburgh woman who was given, as a souvenir of the remotest dwelling in Scotland, a fragment of wood from the broken staircase in the house.

Since the fragment came into her possession, strange things have occurred in her house. Crockery has tumbled to the floor for no apparent reason, knocks and heavy footsteps have been heard from time to time, and on one occasion she caught the smell of strong drink and tobacco before glimpsing the outline of a bearded sailor. She has never visited Sandwood Bay or Sandwood Cottage, and she did not know that the bay, and particularly the cottage, is said to be haunted by the ghost of a bearded sailor who has been seen from time to time by fishermen, shepherds and sailors. An intriguing tale.

An alternative return route to Oldshore Beg is possible by following the cliff tops back from Sandwood Bay. This adds considerably to the distance and the going is very rough with a lot of up and down, but may appeal to stronger and more experienced walkers.

Walk 3
COIRE MHIC FHEARCHAIR OF BEINN EIGHE
HIGHLAND
5 miles

No walking guide to the northern parts of Britain would be complete without at least a reference to Torridon, one of the most scenic parts of this country. I've chosen a walk to what I think is possibly the grandest of all Scottish mountain corries, Coire Mhic Fhearchair. It's a there-and-back rather than circular walk, but the scenery is so impressive I'm sure you won't mind seeing it twice.

If you go to Coire Mhic Fhearchair in the autumn then the surrounding moors and the corrie itself resound to the sound of rutting stags. Don't be fooled into thinking the white summits of these great hills are snow-capped – the quartzite tops of the Torridon mountains tend to be light grey in colour, similar to snow. But by late autumn it could well be snowing on the high tops, and in the depths of winter Coire Mhic Fhearchair is a grand sight indeed with its ice-encrusted buttresses, scalloped cornices above, and the lochan hidden under a mantle of white.

In 1967 the National Trust for Scotland took into its care on behalf of the nation the 14,000 acre estate of Torridon which includes some of the finest mountains in Scotland. The Trust's property includes Liathach and Beinn Alligin, the southern slopes of Beinn Dearg to its skyline, and the southern slopes of Beinn Eighe from the summit ridge of Sail Mhor to Spidean Coire nan Clach. The two principal mountains in the group, Liathach and Beinn Eighe, are outstanding for the grandeur of their corries, crags, pinnacles and

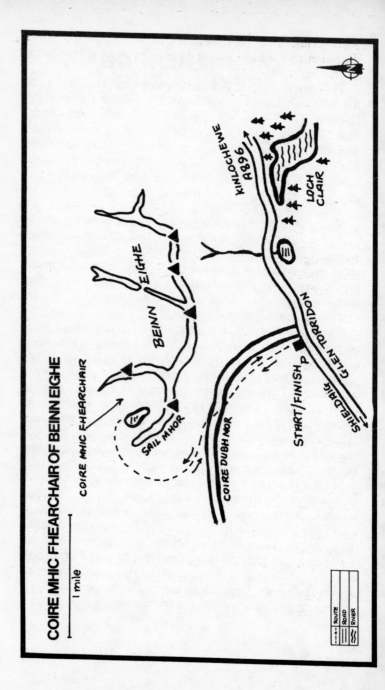

COIRE MHIC FHEARCHAIR OF BEINN EIGHE

1 mile

COIRE MHIC FHEARCHAIR

BEINN EIGHE

SAIL MHOR

COIRE DUBH MOR

START/FINISH P

SHIELDAIG GLEN TORRIDON

KINLOCHEWE A896

LOCH CLAIR

ROUTE
ROAD
RIVER

soaring ridges. The mountains are made from quartz-capped Torridonian sandstone, thought to be the oldest rock in the world, laid down some 750 million years ago.

That part of Beinn Eighe not owned by the National Trust for Scotland is under the care of the Nature Conservancy Council. This covers over 10,000 acres. Beinn Eighe was the first National Nature Reserve to be declared in Britain and was acquired primarily for the preservation and study of the fairly large remnant of Caledonian pinewood. The woodlands are being extended within enclosed areas so that red deer can't graze on the newly formed shoots.

The mountain slopes of Beinn Eighe are of great geological, physiographical and floristic interest. Pine martens are among the animals protected in the reserve as well as wildcat, fox, badger, buzzard and golden eagle. Research work is carried out here from the nearby Anancaun field station. The area displays all the main rocks and there are many Arctic and alpine plants.

The steep-sided valleys and prominent hills are largely the result of glaciation when the ice gouged deep into the sandstone. The result has been superb montane relics like this walk's objective, Coire Mhic Fhearchair, great deeply eroded and ice smoothed hollows. Coire Mhic Fhearchair itself is dominated by a great triple buttress of light grey quartzite which stands on an equally impressive plinth of red sandstone, looming over a rock cradled lochan which spills out over the corrie lip into a series of white falls and cascades.

From the outflow of the lochan a track curves west then south round the base of Sail Mhor to link up with another track in Coire Dubh. The shortest walking route to Coire Mhic Fhearchair is by this track up Coire Dubh. The journey out takes about two and a half hours from the Glen Torridon road and the point where the track branches uphill along the flank of Sail Mhor is marked by a large cairn.

Leave your car in the prominent roadside car park near Slugach, about seven miles west of Kinlochewe on the A896 Kinlochewe to Torridon road. The path is signposted and initially follows the stream called Allt Coire an Anmoich. The

19

Coire Mhic Fhearchair of Beinn Eighe, one of the most exciting corries in the Scottish highlands.

path is a good one and rises gently into the narrow confines of Coire Dubh Mor, the Big Dark Corrie. This is a superb situation, with the great flank of Beinn Eighe on your right, and the castellated buttresses of Liathach on your left – two of the finest mountains in the country.

As you begin to descend from the summit of the pass you'll come across a small lochan beside the track. Just opposite this you'll find the cairn I referred to earlier, so take the right-hand branch of the track and follow it gently uphill in a north-easterly direction around the flanks of Sail Mhor. Below you lie the waters of Loch nan Cabar, and if you stop and look behind you, and the weather is clear, you'll enjoy a tremendous view of the rugged cliffs, buttresses and corries of the north flanks of Liathach, truly a remarkable sight.

The path continues to rise gently and then rather steeply before the grandeur of the Coire Mhic Fhearchair bursts into view.

As you wander round this path, and as you return to Glen Torridon, keep your eyes peeled for some of the fauna of

20

Torridon. Although not numerous, this offers a fine variety, from the red deer, Britain's largest mammal, to the pygmy shrew, its smallest. If you are really lucky you might hear the call of greenshank from one of the hill lochans, or the eerie call of the great northern diver. In September and October these glens reverberate to the sound of the stag rut. Take some binoculars and try and spot one of the stags as it lifts its head back and roars like a great lion. The sound of it is the very epitome of the highland wilderness, a primeval roar. Buzzards may wheel above the roadside, but as you wander up the length of Coire Dubh Mor you're more likely to see an even greater bird of prey, the golden eagle. The golden plover may well entertain you with its melancholy whistle, and higher up towards the Coire Mhic Fhearchair itself you'll possibly hear the gruntings and cackle of grouse and even ptarmigan, the bird of the high tops.

Walk 4
THE VIEW TO THE ISLES
HIGHLAND
8 miles

This fine circular walk, which starts and finishes in the fishing village and ferry port of Mallaig, gives you a superb view out across the harbour towards the outer isles. Mallaig is very much the culmination point of the traditional Road to the Isles. It's here the road ends, and if you want to go further, then it has to be by boat.

It's worthwhile taking this short walk, for the view is unparalleled. The vast seaward panorama encompasses the mountain ranges from south and north, from the distant Point of Ardnamurchan, the most westerly point on the British mainland, to the great horseshoe of the Cuillin hills of Skye, then beyond to the Sound of Sleat and Kintail. In between lie the Small Isles, Rhum of the craggy Cuillin-like mountains, and Eigg and Canna, remarkably flat compared with the mountains that lie all around you.

Especially close to you are the great mountains of Knoydart, that vast wilderness area that lies in a peninsula bounded by Loch Hourn, the Loch of Hell, and Loch Nevis, the Loch of Heaven. Trapped in its mountain limbo, between heaven and hell, Knoydart is a magnificent area that is both roadless and, for the most part, unpopulated.

If the weather is clear, you may well see beyond the Small Isles to the Outer Hebrides – the rocky hills of Harris and the long flat expanse of Lewis – and maybe, if you are exceptionally lucky, even beyond that to lonely St Kilda on the edge of the Atlantic.

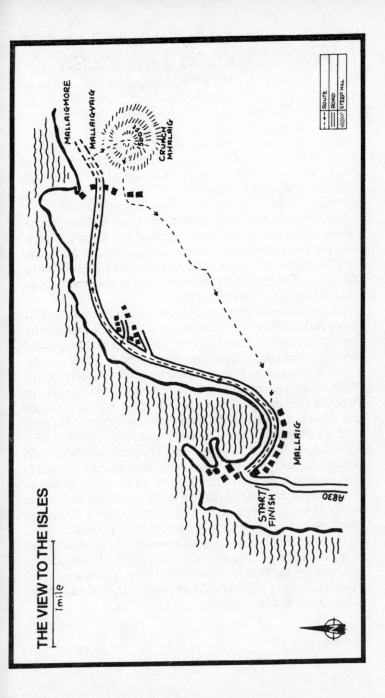

THE VIEW TO THE ISLES

1 mile

MALLAIGMORE

MALLAIGVAIG

CRUACH MHALAIG

500

MALLAIG

START/FINISH

A830

ROUTE
ROAD
STEEP HILL

N

Mallaig lies at the end of the West Highland Railway, the railway journey from Fort William that is claimed to be one of the finest in the country. Yet even better than this sixty mile journey is the train ride from Glasgow. You can sit back and enjoy the scenic delights of Loch Lomondside, the beauty of Strathfillan, and the wide open expanses of the bare Rannoch Moor before the train follows the line of Loch Trieg towards the gorge at Tulloch and the long miles of Glen Spean. Have lunch in Fort William, the capital of the western highlands, and rejoin the train again for its afternoon run along the banks of Loch Eil, to Glenfinnan at the head of Loch Shiel, past Loch an Uamh where Bonnie Prince Charlie left Scotland after his ill-fated attempt at uprising, and on towards the white sands of Arisaig and Morar.

The train stops at Mallaig, and here many people continue their journey out towards the Hebrides, to the Isle of Skye or Rhum, to Eigg and Canna. There are motor-boat cruises, too, to Loch nan Uamh and Loch Moidart, to Loch Scavaig in Skye, to Loch Duich in Kintail and to Loch Hourn in Knoydart. Indeed, if that great wilderness area of Knoydart is your destination, then it's from Mallaig you will sail, across the wide expanse of Loch Nevis to Inverie.

Mallaig is a magical sort of a place. Always busy, it is noisy with the cacophony of gulls, eager to catch a small piece of fish from one of the fishing boats. The harbour is very much the centre of activity. Mallaig is a specialised fishing port, and after fishing all else seems to be ignored. The harbour is the focal point for visitors, too, enjoying the sights and sounds of the fleet, the bustle of landing the catch and despatching it on its way to the south. Fifty herring boats use the harbour, and the lobster fleet fishes two thousand miles of coastline, making Mallaig the most important herring and shellfish port of the west coast. You'll hear the broad brogue of north-east Scotland mix with the gentle softness of the West Highland accents, for each Monday morning the fishing fleet crews arrive from their homes in Aberdeenshire and Banffshire, travelling these great distances to fish the best waters in the country.

The end of the Road to the Isles: the view to the Inner Hebrides and beyond.

The walk starts on the east side of the harbour bay, along a public road which runs for a mile or so above the bay and through a small housing estate. Once clear of the houses the road runs alongside the hillside to the tiny crofting community of Mallaigvaig. Down below you lie the waters of the outer Loch Nevis, and across its silvery expanse the hills of Knoydart lie serene. It was here that Bonnie Prince Charlie landed on his escape from Skye on July 5th, 1746, during his post-Culloden flight from the troops of the government and the Duke of Cumberland.

Beyond Mallaigvaig a track, known locally as the Burma Road, continues for three-quarters of a mile to the croft at Mallaigmore. Half-way along this track, climb the slopes to the fine vantage point of Cruach Mhalaig, where you will be amply rewarded for your efforts by the superb views across to the Small Isles. However, if you don't feel inclined to climb the hill to Cruach Mhalaig, you can still enjoy a fine view of the seascape.

By the public phone box at Mallaigvaig you will see a signpost showing the way back to Mallaig. This fine little path crosses the moorland above the village and finishes in an interesting little valley which takes you back all the way to the main road at the harbour.

All in all an interesting and rewarding walk in the company of gulls, curlews, lapwing and skylark.

Walk 5
ST ABBS WILDLIFE RESERVE
BORDERS
6 miles

St Abbs Wildlife and Nature Reserve is perched on one of the most rugged and precipitous stretches of coastline on the entire east coast of Scotland. It juts out sharply and pointedly, and in rough conditions its sheer cliffs are buffetted by the roaring North Sea almost 300 feet below.

Under joint management of the National Trust for Scotland, who bought it in 1980, and the Scottish Wildlife Trust, the reserve comprises a total of 192 acres of both cliffs and coastal headland, piercing out into the North Sea. The harbour of St Abbs nestles in the shelter of the volcanic rock that dominates the coastline.

The reserve is famous as a breeding ground for a wide variety of seabirds, with kittiwakes, razorbills, fulmars and guillemots flitting in and out of the rock and shoreline. On land, stonechats and wheatears are very much in evidence.

At the west end of the reserve stands St Abbs lighthouse, warning shipping of the dangers of sailing too close to the coastline. The reserve also has a ranger, and it is recommended that large parties in particular should make contact before setting out into the reserve.

St Abbs is served by a bus service from Berwick-upon-Tweed which also passes through Eyemouth and Coldingham. Buses also operate between Edinburgh and Berwick and pass through Coldingham, where the walk begins. It is possible to shorten the walk by about 3¼ miles by starting at the parking and information area at Northfield Farm.

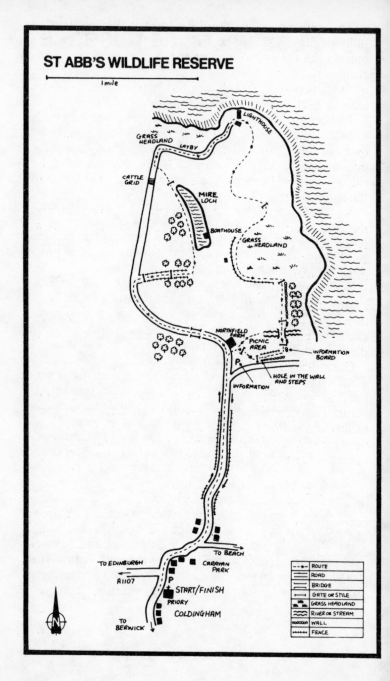

There are a number of parking areas in Coldingham (ten miles up the coast from Berwick), but the walk will begin outside the Priory, which was founded in 1098 by Edgar, King of the Scots, destroyed by Cromwell in 1648, repaired in 1662, restored in 1854, and finally renovated 100 years later in 1954. It is still used for public worship.

The first part of the walk follows the main road which leads to St Abbs, and as the walker climbs out of the village and over the crest of the hill the North Sea and the village come into view, the latter a peaceful haven and favoured by sub-aqua clubs. Its serenity and peace is indeed welcome to the summer visitor from the city.

A path leads down to St Abbs, but you should continue on the main road to a parking area and information kiosk at Northfield Farm. Here, the mixed ingredients of farming and inquisitive visitor have married and blossomed with the influx of naturalist and picnicker.

Marker posts direct you around the outskirts of the farm to a path running parallel to the road to St Abbs, before you turn sharp left at a high wall and then follow the path over a small bridge and through a number of gates before reaching the open headland.

Great care should be taken at all times, particularly if the wind is from the west, as the path on occasions passes close to the rocky coastline. The high cliffs, with their wildlife set in nature's true environment, present some of the most spectacular scenery in the country. On such a high promontory the air is always bracing both in summer and winter. It is not unknown for the whin bushes to be in full bloom in February.

The path at this stage is well defined. It is worth taking time to halt, perhaps taking advantage of a few seats that have been suitably placed, to admire the magnificent panorama and listen to the breakers of the North Sea and the thrilling call of the wildlife.

For a time the path leaves the sight of the sea and passes to the west of Kirk Hill; in the foothills sheep graze, scarcely acknowledging the passing intruder. But it is not long before

29

St Abbs Lighthouse, viewed from the Wildlife Reserve

the sea comes into view again, and the lighthouse. This is private property, and you must pass round the west of the buildings to reach the road, which leads down to Northfield.

Straight ahead, the ocean batters the coast for mile upon mile. Follow the road's twisting route downhill, to reach a cosy inlet at Pettico Wick, with a slipway perhaps holding stories of days of smuggling, now used by divers.

Turn left here – there is no evidence of a distinct track – before reaching a part of the road where it begins to climb and there is a cattle grid. On the left is Mire Loch, a narrow, neat passage of water which boasts numerous wildlife. Cross over a stile and follow a path down the right-hand side of the loch. The path will guide the walker through shrubland and trees, some planted in the memory of a Peter Howard Forster, who, a plaque tells us, 'loved this headland but who was lost in a diving accident in 1981.'

At the end of Mire Loch, which was dammed in 1901, is a boathouse, camouflaged in the trees, its tiled roof showing signs of strain from the strength of the wind that often batters the coast.

At the end of the loch, a track leads uphill to the right, passing a small thicket of trees and through two gates to rejoin the road which began at the lighthouse. On joining the road, turn left and continue on it to reach the cluster of cottages and farm at Northfield. From there, follow the road back to Coldingham.

Walk 6
NEIDPATH CASTLE
BORDERS
5¾ miles

Neidpath Castle, an ancient fortress with a commanding view of the silvery River Tweed one mile west of the Royal Burgh of Peebles, is an outstanding example of a border pele tower. The L-shaped building has been inhabited since the early fourteenth century to the present day. During 1645 the castle was garrisoned against the Marquis of Montrose and in 1650 against the force of Cromwell.

The castle originally belonged to the Hay family, but in 1810 the estate passed to the Earls of Wemyss, and the building is now open to the public under the Wemyss and March Estates.

The castle plays a significant role in the Beltane Festival, an annual event to celebrate the Riding of the Marches, revived in 1897 to commemorate Queen Victoria's Diamond Jubilee. One of the most poignant ceremonies of the week-long celebrations is the installation of the Warden of Neidpath, a ceremony that goes back to 1930. The warden, from the steps of this ancient keep, then addresses the public; among notable persons to have filled this high position are MP David Steel and Lord Lieutenant Col Aidan M. Sprot.

The castle is open from Easter to October.

The walk begins in Peebles, the name of which is derived from the ancient word pebylls (tents) which were pitched there by the wandering Gadeni tribe, the founders of the town. Peebles is served by buses from Edinburgh, Galashiels, and Biggar. The start of the walk is a small car

The lochs of Scotland add a touch of romance (*previous page*).

The high, windswept moors of the Highlands (*above*).

A small burn tumbles off the moor (*right*).

Snow and ice increase the sense of drama and remoteness.

The moors are dotted with deserted buildings (*right*).

Mist descends on Glen Coe.

The dramatic coast of eastern Scotland (*right*).

Early autumn on the moors, the heather providing a carpet
of purple as far as the eye can see.

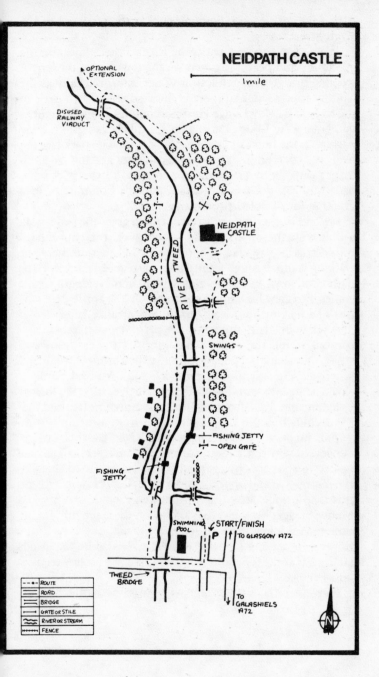

NEIDPATH CASTLE

1 mile

OPTIONAL EXTENSION

DISUSED RAILWAY VIADUCT

RIVER TWEED

NEIDPATH CASTLE

SWINGS

FISHING JETTY
OPEN GATE

FISHING JETTY

SWIMMING POOL

START/FINISH
P
TO GLASGOW A72

TWEED BRIDGE

TO GALASHIELS A72

– ◆ –	ROUTE
	ROAD
	BRIDGE
⊢——	GATE OR STILE
～～	RIVER OR STREAM
⊢⊢⊢⊢	FENCE

N

park adjacent to the swimming pool at the west end of the High Street.

As you leave the car park, the River Tweed, meandering gracefully and peacefully through the town, is on the left. A wooden bridge over Eddleston Water, known locally as the Cuddy, is crossed, and there is then a distinct path close to the river. The Hay Lodge Hospital complex is on the right as you enter Hay Lodge Park, a delightful area of ground and parkland, the home of Peebles rugby club. The park is set in beautiful surroundings with huge oak trees gracing the landscape; with the river famous for anglers, a fishing jetty has been built by Borders Regional Council's Community Programme for disabled fishermen.

Beyond Fotheringham Bridge, which gives the pedestrian a link with the opposite side of the river, the path curves round past a play area to enter a wooded section; here the walking is much rougher until a stile is reached. Beyond, the path cuts down to a wide grassy plain and Neidpath Castle comes into view high up on the right. On the approach to the castle, a narrow path leads up to the entrance gates.

After your visit, return to the path at the riverside and contour round the rocky promontory of the castle, over a stile, and along a wide, winding path through woodland before another stile, leading into a field, is reached. Straight ahead is the famous railway viaduct which carried the former Caledonian railway from Peebles to Symington. It is said that the architect carved his rough model from a turnip.

The main walk now crosses the river by this bridge. However, you can choose to continue another half a mile upstream and cross by the road bridge leading to the head of the impressive and appealing Manor Valley. Having crossed this road bridge, take the first fork on the left over the old Manor bridge, built in 1703; and go up the steep hill, taking time to cast a look back to some of the highest peaks in the Borders, including Dollar Law. A path leads into the woods on the left at the top of the hill, and this can be followed back into Peebles.

However, the main route will cross the earlier railway

34

Neidpath Castle, a perfect example of a Border pele tower

viaduct. As you cross you will see, straight ahead, the boarded-up entrance to the South Park tunnel, which runs almost three-quarters of a mile through the hill. Gangs of Irish labourers built the tunnel in 1863.

On the far side of the viaduct, cross a stile on the left and follow the path downhill to the bank of the river. There are numerous paths, but it is advisable to follow the one closest to the river. The path is rocky in parts and care will need to be taken, particularly in wet weather. A fine view of the castle can be obtained from Artist's Rock, situated at a part of the river known as Gardenfoot. There is much evidence in the castle of the damage caused by Cromwell's cannons which bombarded the fortress from a high point on this side of the river.

At the end of the wood, noted for its wildlife, the path emerges via a stile into a tarmacadam track which leads back to Peebles. The steeple of the old parish church is dominant

35

in the distance but on the right there is now no evidence of the former Caledonian railway station. Peebles at one time had two stations, linked by a loop line, the North British serving the line from Galashiels to Edinburgh.

The river slows, deeper as it approaches the Cauld via a stretch of water known as the Minnie. At the end of the path, turn left onto the road to cross the main Tweed Bridge, originally timber-built and stoneclad. Turn left again at the end of the bridge then descend to the car park.

Walk 7
THE LOST VALLEY OF GLENCOE
HIGHLAND
3 miles

Glencoe is a place of haunting beauty. Certainly not a pretty place, or scenically attractive as, say, Loch Lomondside. Rather, Glencoe has an austerity that, particularly in bad weather, can be almost frightening. Its scenery is on the grand scale and the car-borne tourist is both dwarfed and humbled by the landscape around him.

The objective for this walk lies in the tight clench of surrounding ridges and peaks – a lost valley which provides a haven not only for the walker and climber but for wildlife as well. It is a marvellous place to lie and watch the herds of red deer wander down from the tops, grazing peacefully on the lush grass of the valley basin. In this lost valley I have also spotted a ptarmigan – the mountain grouse, the Arctic species which turns from its usual mottled grey to pure white during the winter months.

If you are lucky, you'll also see in this secluded and very special place eagle, buzzard, and possibly a peregrine falcon. Chaffinches predominate in the birch woods at the lower end of the valley, but higher up you are likely to hear the harsh clacking of a ring ouzel, the mountain blackbird.

As you drive into the jaws of Glencoe from the south, you are immediately aware that this is a pass of note. The road winds on before you, passing one or two small farms amongst tracings of greenery. A loch at the far end of the glen, Loch Achtriochtan, affords some relief from the austere setting, and beyond it the sea begins at Loch Leven.

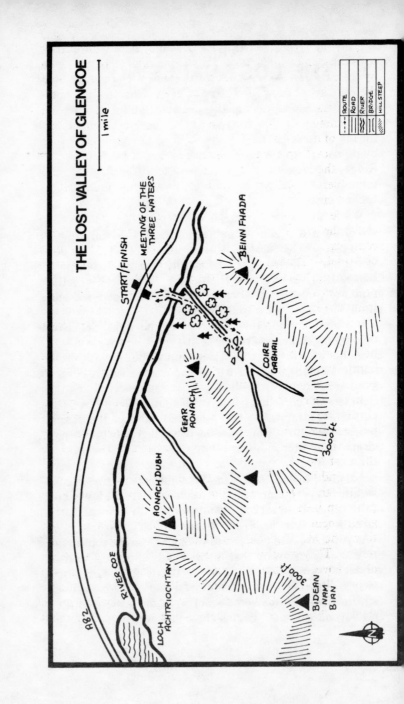

THE LOST VALLEY OF GLENCOE

1 mile

START/FINISH

MEETING OF THE THREE WATERS

BEINN FHADA

COIRE GABHAIL

GEAR AONACH

AONACH DUBH

3000 ft

LOCH ACHTRIOCHTAN

RIVER COE

A82

BIDEAN NAM BIAN

3000 ft

	ROUTE
	ROAD
	RIVER
	BRIDGE
	HILL-STEEP

N

On your right-hand side an imposing mountain barrier seals the glen from the north. It's a great wall, torn and riven by scree runs, narrow gullies which more often than not hold the remains of the winter's snow, even well into July. Frequently the top of this wall is capped by cloud, but if you are lucky enough to arrive there on a clear day you'll notice that the top of this great ridge is crooked, jagged and rough, torn by pinnacles, spires and gullies. This is the Aonach Eagach Ridge, the Notched Ridge, and it offers mountaineers and scramblers a challenging walk along its three mile switchbacked crest.

While the Aonach Eagach creates a continuous barrier along the north side of the glen, the south side is more complex. One great mountain, the highest in the old county of Argyll, is Bidean nan Bian, and it throws out three great fingers into the confines of the pass. Each of these ridges protrudes into the glen in great rock buttresses, and viewed from the top of the glen it's easy to see why they are called the Three Sisters of Glencoe. These are in the most part sheer rock faces; one of them, Aonach Dubh, shows a vertical slit high on its north face. This is Ossian's Cave, named after the bardic warrior son of Finn McCuil, or Fingal as he is generally known in Scotland.

In between these great buttresses lie huge scalloped glacial cirques, known in Scotland as corries. One of them, lying between Beinn Fhada and Gear Aonach, can't be seen very clearly from the road, and is known as the Coire Ghabail, or the Lost Valley.

Legend has it that the MacDonalds of Glencoe, who once lived in the lower stretches of Glencoe, used to hide stolen cattle up here, where they couldn't be spotted by passing government troops. Like most of the highland clans at the time, the MacDonalds were known freebooters and cattle reivers. They were, in fact, a considerable thorn in the flesh of the government at the time, and they consistently refused to pay allegiance to the king of the day, William. Eventually their clan chief, MacIan, did travel south to pay homage to the king, but he arrived too late to prevent orders being sent

High and hidden, the lost valley of Glencoe was once used to hide stolen cattle.

from the government to the garrison stationed at Inverlochy, now known as Fort William, ten miles north of Glencoe. These orders were to 'put all to the sword under ninety'.

The Massacre of Glencoe is remembered even today, not so much as an act of discipline by the government, nor as an inter-clan feud, but because of the way the orders were carried out. Pretending that the garrison at Fort William was overfull, the captain of the regiment who had been given the orders – a Campbell, as were many of the soldiers – told the MacDonalds that the soldiers had to be billeted with the Glencoe families. One night, under cover of dark, the alarm was raised; the soldiers rose and murdered their hosts. Thus the age-old custom of highland hospitality was breached, and the clan Campbell has never been forgiven.

The Lost Valley, then, is well worth a visit in the glen of history. To start the walk, leave the main A82 at the Meeting of the Three Waters and take the obvious footpath down to the gorge formed by the River Coe. A footbridge crosses the river and its rocky gorge, and a footpath climbs up from it to

40

follow the banks of the Allt Coire Gabhail. The path steepens here and there but take your time and enjoy the views back down the length of the glen towards Loch Achtriochtan.

Higher up, the path runs through a deep cleft among birch trees; a marvellous place to be in spring and autumn. Take care as you follow the path now as it waves in and out between rocky outcrops, and eventually crosses the burn to a gravelly path which takes you above the trees to the breathtaking splendour of the upper corrie.

Here lies the great green meadow of the Lost Valley, hemmed in by the steep-sided and jagged ridges of Bidean nam Bian, a direct contrast to the rocky tree-clad route we have just followed. It's to this secluded place that the Macdonalds of Glencoe brought their cattle to graze on the green meadows undisturbed.

Take a walk up the half a mile of the meadow where the stream runs underground, and enjoy the solitude of it all.

Return to the A82 by the same path, but look back up behind you as you go to appreciate just how hidden the valley is.

Walk 8
MEGGET RESERVOIR
BORDERS
4 miles

The Megget valley is long and wide, flanked by steeply rising hills, the tallest of which is Broad Law – at 2,756 feet, the highest south of Edinburgh on the eastern flank of Scotland. Hundreds of years ago, the valley was part of the Forest of Ettrick, a hunting land created by David I, and the country ran with deer for many centuries.

However, this century has witnessed a profound change of landscape. A 184-foot high dam has been built across the valley, stemming the flow of water to form the great tract of Megget reservoir, created to augment the water supply to Edinburgh. Megget valley was chosen as the best site because of its suitable profile, and the fact that it lies close to other reservoirs which serve the capital city. The reservoir, which was inaugurated in 1983, lies in the county of Ettrick and Lauderdale but comes under the auspices of the Lothian region.

The long-term effect on the valley of the creation of the reservoir has been immense. It was to change both the landscape and the old routes of communication of this farming community. No longer able to drive along the floor of the valley, motorists had to take to the new road – from Glengaber to Meggethead – built high above the reservoir. Farms were to disappear under the lapping waters, hidden forever. Before the reservoir was built, over a thousand sheep grazed in the valley. Now only stocked trout glide over the submerged terrain.

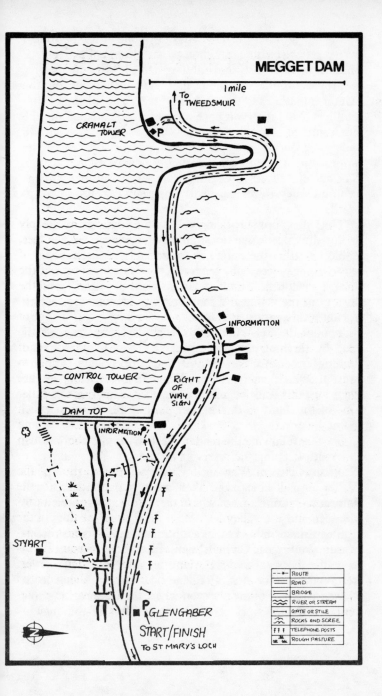

Despite all this, the valley has lost none of its traditional values. New steadings and houses have been built to replace those now drowned, and the new steadings certainly give improved facilities for the farmer and shepherd during the winter months and at lambing time. The planners and builders of the reservoir have successfully blended it into the environment, and it has added its own stamp of character to what was once a grey and desolate place – much of the improvement due to the planting of new trees and shrubs. The ancient towers of Cramalt were saved, and the remains rebuilt as one tower base with superlative views down towards St Mary's Loch.

The valley, not surprisingly, has a high average rainfall; it is equally spectacular in summer and winter, and in the coldest weather the water can freeze over. There are numerous parking places along the top of the dam, and information boards – colourful panels at various vantage points – give the history of the valley and the reservoir. Walkers are catered for by well signposted routes.

Though the area is not served by public transport, access is easy for the motorist. The reservoir lies by the minor road linking Tweedsmuir on the A701 and Cappercleuch (15 miles west of Selkirk) on the A708. Though there is parking on the dam top, this walk begins at Glengaber, a quarter of a mile east of the dam, so this is your parking place and starting point.

Start by following the road to the dam top and continue on the road, keeping the reservoir on the left. You will pass a Scottish Rights of Way Society sign pointing to the Manor Valley near Peebles, and then reach a parking area and information panels from where there are extensive views of the loch and the valley.

Steep-sided hills close in as the road winds its way westwards. Continue to Cramalt, a mile further on the road, at the end of a horseshoe curve round an intensive spur of the reservoir. Just beyond a cottage take the track that leads down to the side of the reservoir where there is a parking area and picnic tables. Here stand the remains of the ancient

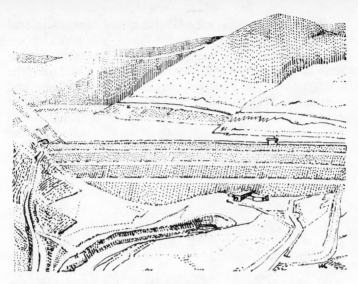

Megget Dam, built to augment Edinburgh's water supply

Cramalt Tower, believed to have been four storeys high at one time.

Retrace your steps to the dam top car park, the return journey giving a new outlook on the reservoir. Across the great stretch of water is Shielhope, draped in trees, and further west the track that leads to Winterhopeburn.

When you reach the dam top, halt a while to learn more about the reservoir from the information panels. Then cross the high face of the dam to the opposite side of the valley to turn left and descend a few steps. Follow the track to a stile and then down through the field to reach another stile which leads onto a farm road. Turn left, cross the bridge, and then turn left again, following the sign marked 'footpaths'.

Go back along the bank of the overflow stream from the dam tower; cross to the right and over a stile to reach the road which leads into the chamber of the dam. It is possible to visit this chamber by prior arrangement with Lothian Regional Council.

Continue straight ahead over two stiles before turning left onto a track. On the right is an Ordnance Survey triangulation point. Follow the track to reach another stile, situated next to the dam top. Turn right and walk down back to the road to Glengaber, your starting point.

Walk 9
WANLOCKHEAD LEAD MUSEUM
STRATHCLYDE
6 miles

At an altitude of 1531 feet, Wanlockhead is the highest village in Scotland and at one time, along with neighbouring Leadhills, it was a thriving lead mining community. The area's importance depended on deposits of gold and silver as well as lead, and it is said that on one occasion a nugget of gold weighing five ounces was found at Wanlockhead.

Although lead mining ceased many years ago, the remains of the industry are still very much in evidence today. The Wanlockhead Museum Trust set up a museum in the village to relate with a high degree of realism the history of an industry which meant valuable jobs for this tiny Strathclyde community. It is also possible to travel undergound to visit one of the mines and experience the conditions under which the workers earned their living.

The route will take you from Leadhills over rough country to Wanlockhead, returning via the course of the former railway line, opened from Elvanfoot to Leadhills in 1901, and to Wanlockhead the following year, to carry lead from the mines to the central belt of Scotland. After the demise of the mines, the line closed eventually as well, but it had continued to be used by both freight and passenger traffic until 1938. However, at the time of writing there is a revival in railway preservation, and the Lowthers Railway Society have plans to reopen the line from Leadhills to Wanlockhead as a tourist attraction. A station building and engine shed are planned for Leadhills.

WANLOCKHEAD LEAD MUSEUM

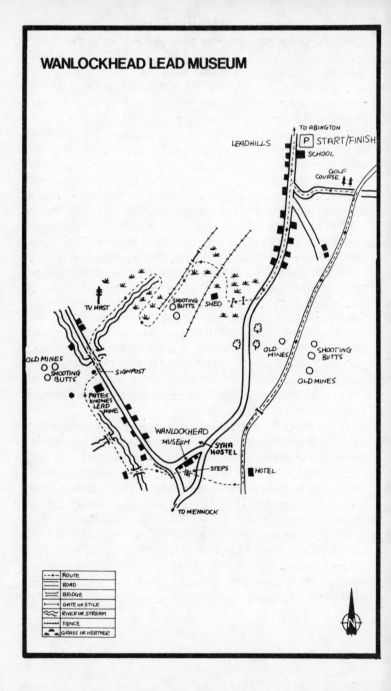

This walk starts at the appropriately-named Leadhills. This village lies at the junction of three minor roads: the B797 and the B7040 (both leading south-west from the A74, and the B797 (leading north-east from the A76, nine miles north of Thornhill). There is parking opposite the police station in the main street and adjacent to the school. A post bus operates in the area, but there is no public transport to it.

Because of their height above sea-level, both villages can be subject to much wetter and colder weather than that of the valleys, and mist can often shroud the hills. If the weather forecast is bad, do not undertake this walk unless you are an experienced and well equipped hill walker with a large-scale map and a compass – and the ability to use both.

Leadhills is a quaint village – in the churchyard is the grave of John Taylor who died at the grand old age of 137. One can study the records of the lead mines in the local library.

From the car park, turn left and walk along the main street towards Wanlockhead. Leave the village, and shortly after passing the de-restriction signs take the path that leads to the right from the road. Follow this path through two sets of gates, set close together; pass a shed on your left and follow the path until a third gate is reached. Go through, and the path winds its way gently uphill to reach a fourth gate – don't go through this one.

Turn left here and follow the fence along the ridge, now at a height of almost 2,000 feet. This is rounded hill country with a base of grass and heather and stupendous views to the Lowther Hills. Continue through the heather along a track which is not always distinct, keeping close to the fence. Another fence comes in from the right, but continue straight ahead until the fence takes a sharp turn down to the left. This leads back to the road, providing an 'escape route' if the weather is foul.

Where the fence turns sharp left, cross over it and follow a narrow path to the edge of the ridge; far below will be seen the lead mines and a cemetery. Now fork right and join a path which swings round the head of the valley. Contour round to follow the ridge on the right of the valley, heading towards

Lochnell Mine, part of the lead museum complex

the old lead mines. You will soon reach a television mast;
from here descend steeply to the road where it passes the
cemetery.

Turn left to follow the road until a signpost indicating the
Southern Upland Way, the long-distance footpath from
Portpatrick to Cockburnspath, is reached. Turn right and
follow the markers. On the left are the restored remains of
part of the Pates Knowes smelt mill, which operated from
1764 to 1845. It has been excavated and conserved for the
museum trust by a job creation team.

Continue to follow the markers of the Southern Upland
Way to reach another indicator point which features a draw-
ing by John Clerk of Eldin, in 1775, of the waterwheel
pumping engine of the Strait Steps mine. Shortly on the left
is the entrance to the Lochnell Mine, and tickets are obtainable from the museum for an escorted tour. Both mine and

50

museum are open from Easter to September. Keep straight ahead to reach the museum close to the road junction. There is a picnic table here, and one can sit alongside two old wagons that once carried the lead from the mines.

After visiting the museum, go up the steps on the Southern Upland Way, cross the road that leads to the Mennock Pass, and continue to the former railway station at Wanlockhead.

Turn left here onto the trackbed of the old railway and cross over the road that leads to the radar station on the Lowther Hills. Pass through a narrow, rocky cutting, and continue over a stile to reach a straight stretch of the old track that leads past mines on either side. Go past a large house on the left and then the site of the old station to enter a second cutting. This will bring you out at a road adjacent to the golf course.

Turn left and follow the road down into the village. At the main street fork right and walk along the road to the car park.

Walk 10
GRETNA GREEN
DUMFRIES & GALLOWAY
$4\frac{1}{2}$ miles

Gretna Green has become famous down the years for the many runaway marriages once conducted there. Young couples, barred by law from marrying south of the border, could, after spending two weeks of seclusion in Scotland, be married over the blacksmith's anvil without the consent of their parents.

English couples had to be 21 years of age before they could marry in their own country. But with Gretna only a few miles over the border north of Carlisle, it was comparatively easy for them to elope and be married there.

It was at Gretna Hall Hotel, built in 1710, that such 'marriages of declaration' took place, and, later, in the smithy. The young couple concerned required two witnesses, and when they returned to their own country their marriage was accepted as legal and binding.

Many youngsters were pursued over the border by their parents who would try to annul the marriages. Yet by law in Scotland these were legal and there was nothing the parents could do after the couple had had their marriage vows affirmed over the anvil. Quite often couples would arrive during the night and arouse the blacksmith from his bed requesting to be married. Without question he would perform the ceremony there and then, and the couple could return home as man and wife.

Marriages at Gretna go back as far as 1792. Over the years the famous anvil has been associated with thousands of

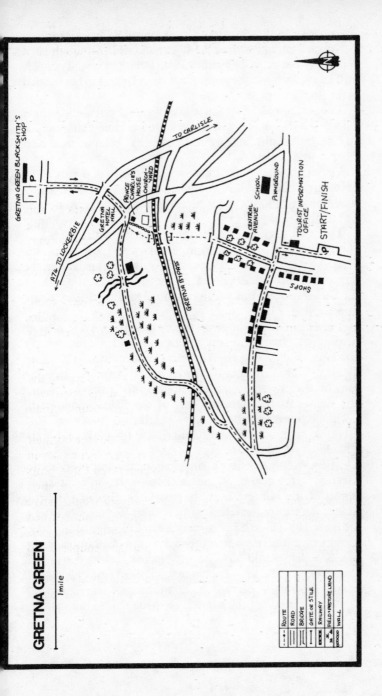

GRETNA GREEN

1 mile

GRETNA GREEN BLACKSMITH'S SHOP

A74 TO LOCKERBIE

TO CARLISLE

PRINCE CHARLIE'S HOUSE

CHURCH-YARD

GRETNA HOTEL HALL

GRETNA BYPASS

CENTRAL AVENUE

SCHOOL

PLAYGROUND

TOURIST INFORMATION OFFICE

START/FINISH

SHOPS

	ROUTE
	ROAD
	BRIDGE
	GATE OR STILE
	RAILWAY
	FIELD-PASTURE LAND
	WALL

marriages. One blacksmith by the name of Richard Rennison performed no fewer than 5,147 ceremonies. Although such marriages ceased to be legal in 1940, over a thousand couples still go each year to the register office in Gretna to be married – the appeal remains.

Today the old blacksmith's shop has been transformed into a visitors' centre, and to meet present time's commercial demand the Auld Smiddy restaurant has been opened next door to the centre.

Visitors to the centre today are greeted by a piper, and a favourite photograph is one taken by the anvil in a jocular wedding ceremony. The centre is open from March to September.

The walk begins in the village of Gretna, which is split by the main trunk A74 road from Glasgow to Carlisle and the Gretna by-pass. There is a car park about 50 yards from the Tourist Information Centre in the middle of the village. There are public bus services from Dumfries, Longtown, and Carlisle.

Turn right out of the car park and walk diagonally through a park with swings to reach the main road. Cross over the road and walk along the attractive, and graceful tree-lined Central Avenue, to another road. Cross this and go through a gate on the opposite side. Continue on the path that bisects the fields. At the opposite side of the field go under the Gretna by-pass and the railway, which runs from Carlisle to Glasgow via Dumfries and Kilmarnock, formerly part of the Caledonian Railway.

The coming of the railway had major implications for Gretna. In the beginning the Caledonian station was situated south of the border; later, Gretna Green became the first station on part of the Glasgow and South Western Railway to be served by a North British service from Longtown. Today, expresses pound their way through Gretna without stopping – a fact that would have been welcomed when the railway came to Gretna as there were complaints of this having resulted in a big increase in the number of marriages.

At the far end of the tunnel, go through another gate and

Gretna Green, famous for runaway marriages

follow the path that goes slightly right towards a cemetery.
Go along beside the wall to reach another road. Cross this and
take the road that goes virtually straight ahead. Pass under
the A74 road, and after 100 yards you will reach the white-
walled visitor centre and blacksmith's shop.

Take some time while at the centre to also see the coach
museum which contains superb examples of coaches similar
to those once used by elopers. You can also see a display of
farm implements.

On leaving the centre, go back down the road under the
A74 to reach the junction. Turn right, and then take the road
that leads to the left. Continue on this road, passing on a
gentle bend a farm on the right. You will soon cross over the
railway before coming down to reach the by-pass. Take care
while crossing this busy road.

Once across, go right for a few yards before turning left
onto a quiet road that will bring you back into the centre of
Gretna. The beginning of the Solway can easily be seen,
while on a clear day the 3,000 foot mountain of Skiddaw in
the Lake District dominates the distant skyline.

Walking back into Gretna one can appreciate the benefits

the by-pass has brought to the town – no more heavy juggernauts thundering through the centre. At the bottom of Central Avenue turn right and return to the car park.

Walk 11
LOCH AN EILEAN – LOCH OF THE ISLAND
HIGHLAND
7 miles

Loch an Eilean, with its island castle, is one of the best-known and most loved beauty spots in the Highlands of Scotland. For the author, it is the most picturesque loch in Scotland, with its backdrop of heather clad mountains, ancient pine forest and craggy skyline. It lies like a jewel amid the splendour of the Rothiemurchus Forest, a priceless natural asset of ancient Caledonian pine which once offered shelter to bears, wolves, lynx and great elk. Nowadays, particularly around Loch an Eilean, the naturalist can enjoy the sight and sounds of crossbills, crested tits, siskin, green-shank and if he is lucky, the exciting view of an osprey diving for trout.

Loch an Eilean's chief claim to fame is a castle which is built on a tiny island just off the north-western shore. This ancient keep dates from the fourteenth century and was once a stronghold of the mighty Norman family of Comyns, the Lords of Badenoch. It is also thought that the castle was once used by the Wolf of Badenoch, one Alexander Stewart, the bastard son of Robert II of Scotland. This rogue gained his nickname after burning down Elgin Cathedral, the abbot of which had criticised him for having an affair. For his troubles he was excommunicated from the Catholic Church and more or less outlawed.

Today the castle is a ruin, grown over with ivy and birch trees. It faces the north-western shore of the loch with a blank wall which contains one open door. There are stepping stones

57

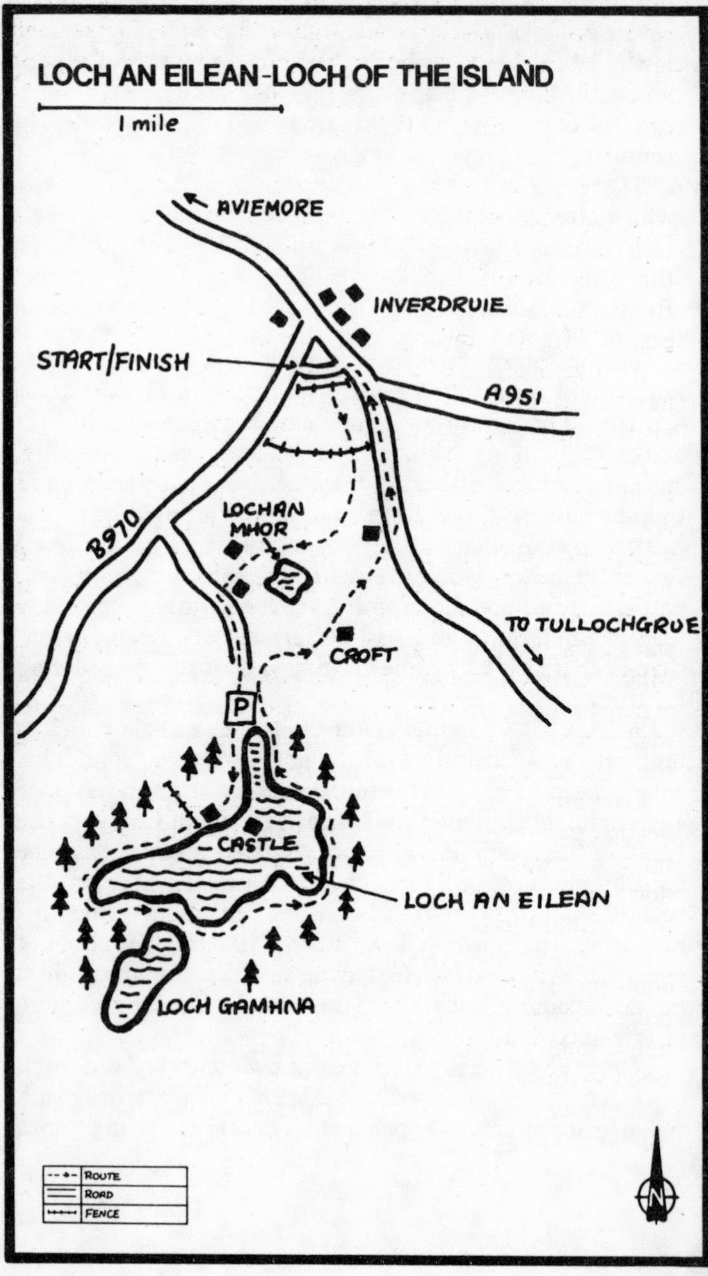

LOCH AN EILEAN - LOCH OF THE ISLAND

1 mile

AVIEMORE

INVERDRUIE

START/FINISH

A951

B970

LOCHAN MHOR

TO TULLOCHGRUE

CROFT

P

CASTLE

LOCH AN EILEAN

LOCH GAMHNA

ROUTE
ROAD
FENCE

N

out to the island, but these can only be seen in periods of severe drought, when the level of the loch water is extremely low. The castle ruins once gave a home to a pair of ospreys who built their eyrie on the walls, but constant attention by egg collectors harassed them greatly and they left earlier this century.

There is a car park at the north end of Loch an Eilean, which offers easy access to a nature trail which encircles the loch (three miles), but if time is available it is far better to link the walk around the loch with a longer walk through Rothiemurchus from Inverdruie, one and a half miles south-east of Aviemore on the A951 Glenmore road.

At Inverdruie, the Rothiemurchus Estate Ranger Service have an Information Centre which would be well worth visiting before setting out for Loch an Eilean.

Across the road from the Information Centre, there is a triangle of roads formed at the junction of the B970 and the A951. On the south side of this triangle an obvious gate gives access through some trees onto moorland. Follow this path for just over half a mile until it is joined by another, wider, track coming in from the left. Continue on this combined track for about 500 yards until you reach the banks of Lochan Mhor, the Big Lochan. This very scenic spot is a water fowl sanctuary where such species as tufted duck, little grebe and mallard can be seen in season. In early summer the edges of the loch are covered in water lilies.

Continue along the track in a westerly direction through heather moorland. This is a good place for spotting roe deer, the smaller deer of the forests, and, in winter, red deer driven down from the high tops by the wind and snow to search for food within the forest.

Soon you will pass a small cottage on your right, and then another on your left. Go through the cottage gate here, remembering to close it behind you, and turn left onto a minor public road. Follow this for just over half a mile to Loch an Eilean.

A nature trail runs around the loch for three miles – easy walking in magnificent surroundings. Much of the forest is

Loch an Eilean, arguably the most attractive loch in Scotland.

old Caledonian pine, gnarled red trees which seem to characterise this part of the highlands. Look out for the birds of the pine forest, and for red squirrels who live here in great numbers. If you're really lucky you might even spot a pine marten, a creature who is re-colonising this part of Speyside after being almost extinct.

At the head of the loch, another narrow trail strikes off to the right. If you have time this is worth following, for it will take you around the small but beautiful Loch Gamhna, the Loch of the Stirks, or young cattle. This reed-fringed loch is seldom visited, and offers a tranquility rarely found in busy Speyside.

Continue with your walk around Loch an Eilean back to the car park at the northern end of the loch. There is another Information Centre here which also sells postcards, sweets and soft drinks.

For the return to Inverdruie continue down the public

road from the car park for about 150 yards. Take the rough road that leads off to the right up a short rise and follow this on past some rough pasture land. There will probably be cattle grazing here, for Rothiemurchus is well known in farming circles for its beef herds.

Soon you will pass a large house, called the Croft, on your right, and another one will be seen through the trees on your left. After a distance another house, Black Park, will appear on your left and here you join the public road which has come down from the right from Whitewell. Follow this road back to Inverdruie.

Walk 12
THE LAIRIG GHRU VIEW
HIGHLAND
8 or 10½ miles

The pass of the Lairig Ghru, the Gloomy Pass, is one of the classic high-level passes in Scotland. It cuts through the great massif of the Cairngorms, a great cleft caused by glaciation, with the bulk of Ben MacDhui on one side and Braeriach on the other – Britain's second and third highest hills respectively. The route itself, from Coylumbridge near Aviemore through the Cairngorms' heartland to Braemar in the south, is some 30 miles in length and rises to a height of over two and a half thousand feet. Such a walk is, of course, outwith the scope of this book, but a superb walk can be enjoyed through the magnificent forest of Rothiemurchus, up through the ancient remains of the Caledonian Pine Forest to the mouth of the Lairig Ghru where there are superb views back over the forest, across Glenmore towards the rising swell of the Monadh Liath hills.

Rothiemurchus is the name of the parish which lies between the River Spey and the summits of the high Cairngorms. Because of the variety of landforms contained in the estate the landscape passes from low-lying fields and hard woods around the fast-flowing rivers, through open moorland ablaze with purple heather in the autumn, through mixed woodland, forestry plantations and the remnants of the Caledonian Pine Forest. Beyond this swell the great rounded domes of the Cairngorms.

The early history of the area was varied and colourful, and its ownership passed through the hands of Comyns, Gor-

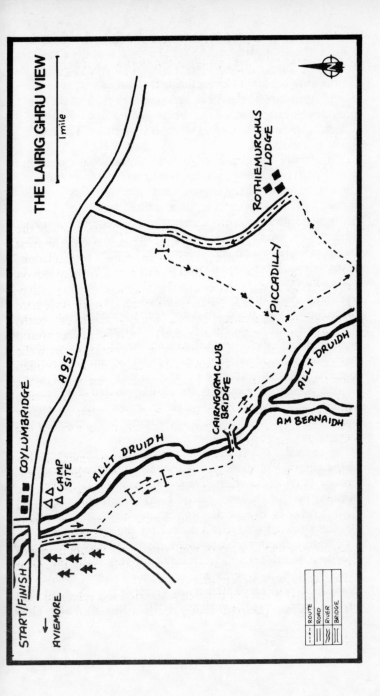

dons, Shaws and McIntoshes before settling in those of Patrick Grant of Muckerach, the second son of the Chief of Grant in 1580.

Our walk begins at Coylumbridge, about two miles south-east of Aviemore on the A951. A lay-by at the side of the road provides parking space. Take the footpath which runs alongside the camping ground and which is signposted 'The Lairig Ghru'.

Right away the character of Rothiemurchus imposes on you. You'll pass a small cottage on the left and from then on there is no more habitation until Rothiemurchus Lodge, owned by the Joint Services, many miles away. Already you are in rich woodland, with a deep and luxuriant undergrowth of bracken, birch scrub and juniper. The red deer are comparatively few on this side of the Cairngorms, and the undergrowth has a good chance to regenerate without being chewed away.

After a short distance you'll come to a fork in the path. Take the left path past a large stone cairn which indicates the Lairig Ghru. Cross the clearing with dense juniper bushes on your right before crossing a stream and heading back into the woodlands. Another stream is crossed by an old railway sleeper, and the next mile or so is through a fairly young conifer plantation. Compare the closely planted commercial conifers with the next stretch of the walk, ancient Caledonian Pine, and you'll realise just how far removed from a natural environment our forests have become.

As you leave the young plantation behind, the first tanta-lising glimpses of the higher hills come into view: the great craggy cliffs of Luchers Crag, or Creag an Leth-Choin, forming one of the jaws of the Lairig Ghru and the Sron Lairig ridge of Braeriach forming the other. In front, the conical shape of Carn Elrig dominates the scene.

What an area this is for wild life. If you're lucky you'll spot roe deer, red deer and squirrels, and if very lucky possibly wild cat, fox, and perhaps even a pine marten, making a comeback to this area after many years absence. Stop at the Iron Bridge across the river where the Allt Druidh and the

Lairig Ghru: the view from one of Scotland's best-known mountain passes.

Am Beanaidh meet and see if you can spot dippers, those dapper little birds that dive into the waters of these fast-flowing streams and search for food on the river beds. You'll recognise it by its dark appearance and white bib. Cross the bridge and continue along the footpath, through some open ground where there lie some ancient ruins, and around a bend to the meeting of the ways.

This is the spot known locally as Piccadilly on account of the paths going in various directions. Our route lies upwards, past the signpost which points you in the direction of the Lairig Ghru and Braemar. This is a superb path, climbing steadily up through the pines. Notice how the pines become shorter and more stunted as you climb. Gradually we leave the forest habitat behind and enter an area of glacial moraine, the rubbish churned up and left by the great glaciers as they carved their way through these big hills. Continue on the path with the Lairig Ghru pass immediately in front. On an overcast day you'll understand why it was called the Gloomy Pass. The sides are steep and scree clad, the very epitome of a mountain pass.

In a short time you'll reach a signpost pointing out Rothiemurchus Lodge, off to the left, so now is a good time to stop for a break and enjoy the view. From here you can gaze across the canopy of trees towards the distant Monadh Liath hills and those beyond. On a fine day Ben Wyvis, beyond Inverness, stands out clearly.

If you wish to keep the total walk length to about eight miles, then turn back at this point and retrace your steps. If you have the time and energy to continue for an extra two and a half miles, there is a detour which you can now follow past Rothiemurchus Lodge.

The path round towards Rothiemurchus Lodge is often muddy after bouts of rain, but the worst of it can be avoided. Rothiemurchus Lodge is a training school run by the Joint Services, and a Land Rover track leads downhill from it back towards Glenmore. It's a typical Joint Services track, built as though to take tank regiments rather than the occasional Land Rover. Aesthetically it's totally displeasing and unnecessary but you don't have to suffer it for long, for after a mile or so you turn back into the forest over a stile in the deer fence on the left, and back down the track to Piccadilly. From there, follow your earlier track back down through Rothiemurchus to Coylumbridge.

Walk 13
CASTLE POINT
DUMFRIES & GALLOWAY
5 miles

Today the Solway Coast is best known for its sands and mudflats where the tides ebb and flow in dangerous mood; yet in days gone by holiday resorts such as Rockcliffe and Kippford enjoyed a different kind of fame, being havens for the smuggler. This walk explores the haunts of those smugglers as well as visiting much earlier sites.

The walk will take you from Kippford along the coast and cliffs to Castle Point, the site of an ancient fort dating from 400 BC, with magnificent views over the Solway. On a clear day, England's Lake District and Cumbrian towns of Maryport and Whitehaven can be seen, seemingly only an arm's distance away.

Set high up on a cliff with a sheer drop towards the sea, Castle Point marks the extremity of this walk, although it is possible to continue on the footpath as far as Sandyhills. However, this entails a rather unexciting return by road.

In comparison with Rockcliffe, Castle Point can be cold and windy, taking as it does the full brunt of the winds that sweep in from the sea. Nevertheless, it offers a superb vantage point.

The walk, part of which crosses land owned by the National Trust for Scotland, visits one of the most famous archaeological sites in southern Scotland at the Mote of Mark, given to the Trust by John and James McLellan in 1937 in memory of their brother, the late Col. William McLellan, and the grave of smuggler Joseph Nelson.

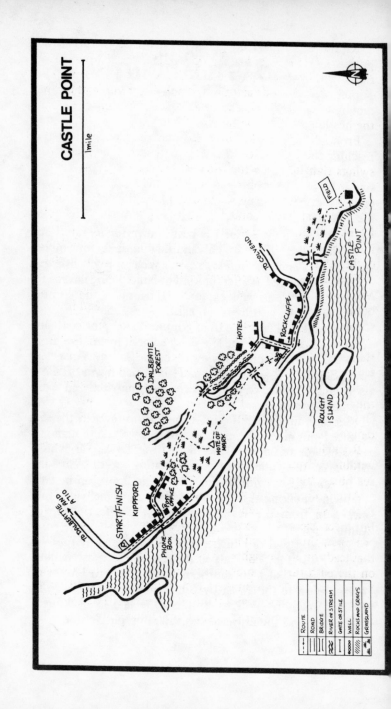

CASTLE POINT

1 mile

N

Legend:
- ...... ROUTE
- ——— ROAD
- ——— BRIDGE
- ≈≈≈ RIVER OR STREAM
- ——I—— GATE OR STILE
- ○○○○ WELL
- ///// ROCKS AND CRAGS
- ⋏⋏⋏ GRASSLAND

TO DALBEATTIE AND A110

START/FINISH

KIPPFORD

PHONE BOX

POST OFFICE

DALBEATTIE FOREST

HOTEL OF MACK

HOTEL

ROCKCLIFFE

TO COLVEND

FIELD

CASTLE POINT

ROUGH ISLAND

Kippford, the starting point of the walk, is served by public transport from Dalbeattie, and lies four miles south of that town. Motorists should take the A710 from Dalbeattie; Kippford is reached via a minor road to the right, and for the motorist there is parking at the entrance to the village next to the headquarters of the Solway Yacht Club.

From the car park, turn left into the village, and on reaching the post office turn left up the hill. The road then swings right to reach the Muckle Lands and Jubilee Path, five and a half acres of rough coastline. Here the tarred road ends and the path begins. This area, under the jurisdiction of the National Trust, offers splendid views over to Rough Island, which is a bird sanctuary. You are advised not to visit it in May or June when the birds are nesting. Also, make sure of the tides before attempting to visit the island at low water.

The path goes along the top of the headland; on the left is Mark Hill in the Dalbeattie Forest. A number of seats have been placed here, and it is worth stopping to admire the scenery, casting an eye to the village of Kippford.

The path winds its way through gorse and broom to reach the edge of the forest. On the right is the Mote of Mark, which you will visit on the return journey. Continue straight ahead along a narrow and pretty lane to reach the roadway at the top of Rockcliffe. Turn right down the hill, and at the shore turn left to follow the road along in front of some delightful homes.

Rockcliffe, like Kippford, is a haven for the visitor and wildlife enthusiast, for the coast is home to a wide variety of sea birds, from redshanks to oystercatchers.

After 250 yards, the walker will reach a road branching off to the right and marked 'The Merse'. This is a private road, but gives access to the footpath that leads to Castle Point.

Follow this road and join the footpath, marked by a sign, that leads off to the right. Go over a footbridge and continue on the path through more gorse and bushes. The path has been renovated by volunteers with support from the Countryside Commission for Scotland, the Scottish Rights of Way Society, and a number of private individuals.

Rockcliffe, a picturesque village on the Solway coast

The path continues close to the shore, and on approaching the last house actually goes down onto the sand and gravel beach. After passing the last house, the path swings round to reach the grave of Joseph Nelson, who came from Workington. He was drowned in a shipwreck in 1791; the stone was erected by his widow.

Continue on the path, cross over a stone stile, and follow the path round the edge of a field to reach a gate and the final climb to Castle Point. Here is a very informative indicator board identifying the surrounding landmarks.

Retrace your steps back to Rockcliffe. Turn left past the car park, cross the road, go through a narrow lane, and into the area known as the Mote of Mark. Go halfway across a field diagonally and then turn slightly left to cross a footbridge. Go straight ahead to reach a noticeboard at the foot of the Mote of Mark.

This site was excavated in 1913 and again in 1973. Fragments of baked clay moulds suggested a casting in metal of Celtic brooches, and pieces of glass of Mediterranean origin also suggested ninth-century occupation.

Turn left to go to the top of the Mote, and then descend by the path leading off from the right. This path continues slightly right, crossing other paths, to the edge of the forest once again. Turn left on the path followed earlier, go past two seats, and then take the track down to the left, through scrub and trees, to reach a wall. Go down between houses to reach the shoreline. Turn right and follow this road back to the car park.

Walk 14
ST NINIAN'S CAVE
DUMFRIES & GALLOWAY
3 miles

Although by necessity this is not a circular walk, it will take you back into the history of the early days of Christianity in southern Scotland. An additional bonus is that part of your route will take you through the delightful Physgill Glen.

Your objective on this walk is St Ninian's Cave, which pierces into the seashore rock on the south coast of an area lying west of Burrow Head known as the Machars. It is situated close to Port Castle Bay in one of several inlets protected by the high cliffs that dominate this jagged coastline.

The peninsula whose rock houses the cave is a typical feature of the Solway coast south-west of the Isle of Whithorn. On this island, St Ninian's Chapel marks the spot at which the Christian pilgrims might possibly have arrived by sea. St Ninian was closely associated with early Christianity in the fifth century. Not a great deal is known about this mysterious missionary except that he did have associations with the south of Scotland – as witnessed by the cathedral priory at Whithorn, and the nearby chapel.

St Ninian's aim was to preach the gospel of Christianity to the inhabitants of this south-western corner. Although a monastery was created at Whithorn which became the focal point for Christians over the years, it was only in 1821 that an incised cross was found at the chapel thus establishing a link with St Ninian. In due course, other crosses were also found, and in 1884 there were major excavations at the cave. A major

ST NINIAN'S CAVE

1 mile

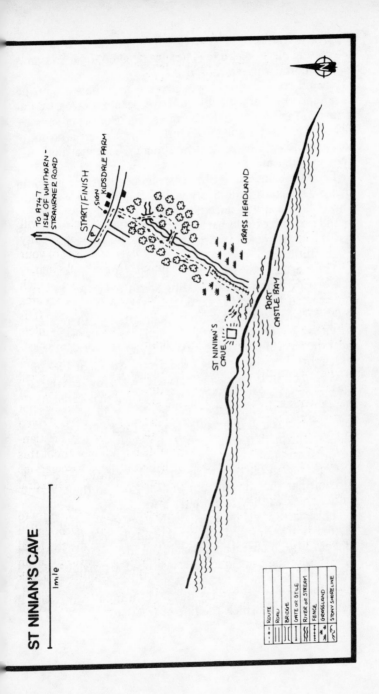

To A747
ISLE OF WHITHORN –
STRANRAER ROAD

START / FINISH
SIGN
KIDSDALE FARM

GRASS HEADLAND

ST NINIAN'S CAVE

PORT CASTLE BAY

	ROUTE
	ROAD
	BRIDGE
	GATE or STILE
	RIVER or STREAM
	FENCE
	GRASSLAND
	STONY SHORELINE

discovery was that of crosses cut in boulders as well as interesting pieces of stone. These were taken to the museum at Whithorn, well worth a visit.

Several crosses were discovered cut into the walls of the cave, and these are thought to have been engraved by pilgrims on their visits to these shores. Some of the crosses are believed to date back to the eighth century. There is no doubt in the minds of experts that St Ninian's Cave was a popular spot for pilgrims.

The cave comes under the auspices of the Ancient Monuments Division of the Scottish Development Department, and although it was once possible to enter the cave, it was found necessary to close it following a rockfall. At the time of writing it was not known whether it would be reopened or not in the future.

The starting point for the walk, near Physgill House, is reached by a minor road leading south from the A747 one mile east of that road's junction with the A746. There is no public transport to the starting point, though there are bus services to Whithorn, further inland. Drive to the car park near the farm of Kidsdale; the walk is signposted from there – a delightful ramble through the pretty woods of Physgill.

Go out of the car park and turn left. Walk towards the farm and take the narrow track down to the right that leads into the wood. Do not follow the road marked private. These are private woods and the walker is privileged to have access to the cave through them. Therefore, please make sure to keep to the path at all times.

Continue on the path to the spot where it divides over the stream that runs down from Ersock Loch to the sea. Take either track as they rejoin after a further 50 yards.

This narrow glade, laced with trees and bursting with daffodils in spring and autumnal plants later in the year, is a delightfully colourful approach to the coast. The trees which line the avenue hang gracefully overhead to provide a canopy through which the sun sparkles on a summer's day – truly a world apart from everyday bustle. Continue on the path to reach a gate, at which the line of trees stops.

St Ninian's Cave, focal point for early Christians

Go straight ahead on the track that is now grassy; the waves of the Atlantic will be seen breaking gently on the Solway coastline. The path is still hemmed in, but gradually it opens out as you near the shoreline. Turn right on the 'beach', which is well endowed with stone. Look straight ahead and you will see the cave of St Ninian standing beneath the distant headland.

Walk along the shore to reach the approach to the cave – there is a track on the right round the huge boulders. Take care if the rocks are wet after rain or soaked by spray from the sea.

The cave is set back into the rock. An information board gives a brief history of the site, telling the visitor that in 1950 it was confirmed as having a long history of occupation dating back to at least the eighth century and that inside the walls have been inscribed by the pilgrims.

75

Take time to view the coastline from the cave before returning to the car park by the same route.

Walk 15
CULZEAN CASTLE & COUNTRY PARK
STRATHCLYDE
6 miles

Culzean Castle and its surrounding country park consti-
tute what estate agents would undoubtedly term a prize site.
There can surely be a no more superlative position than
where it stands on the banks of the Firth of Clyde, looking
across to the beautiful island of Arran, and in the distance, on
a clear day, the coastline of Ireland.

Culzean is a large feather in Ayrshire's cap, and one has to
acknowledge the prominent part it plays in that county's
economy and, in a broader context, in Scotland's heritage.
The castle and country park draw around 300,000 visitors
each year – very much a Scottish jewel. It is owned by the
National Trust for Scotland, who made the acquisition in
1945. Since then the castle and the estate have been restored,
offering the visitor the opportunity to see one of the country's
grandest heirlooms.

At one time the estate and castle belonged to the Marquis
of Ailsa, but the castle is probably now most famous for the
guest flat which became a home for the former American
president Dwight D. Eisenhower. This has helped to forge
strong links between Culzean and the United States, and
Americans flock here in their thousands each year.
Eisenhower first visited Culzean in 1946. Less than a year
before, the National Trust had launched an appeal which
raised £20,000 in six months – a major effort forty years ago.

The castle was opened to the public in 1947. In the first
year visitors totalled 6,000; two years later this had jumped to

CULZEAN CASTLE & COUNTRY PARK

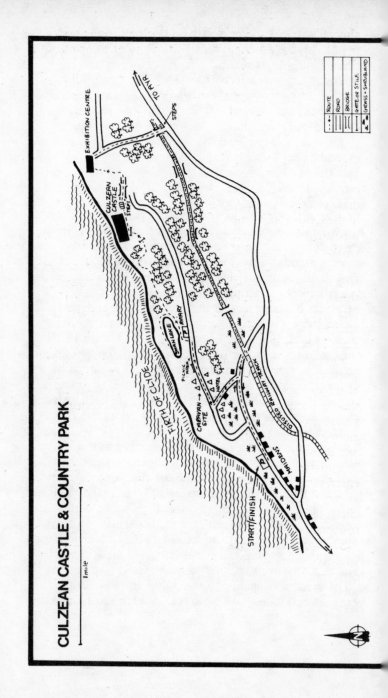

1mile

almost 50,000. Culzean was soon to climb to the top of the popularity poll, having branched out to encompass something for all the family.

Today Culzean offers a breathtakingly beautiful country park allied with a rugged coastline and the freedom to roam around its many attractions. The castle is open from Easter to October and the grounds are open all year round.

There are ample parking areas at Culzean within the grounds. Bus services from Ayr to Turnberry and Girvan pass the main entrance. But this walk begins in the picturesque village of Maidens, south of Culzean, from where the massive rock of Ailsa Craig can be seen standing dominantly in the Clyde. Drive into Maidens on the A719 from Ayr and turn right by the shore to a parking area facing the Firth of Clyde.

Leave the car park and continue on the narrow road which fronts the narrow beach in a north-easterly direction. Ignore the first road leading off to the left, and continue to the next junction where there is an old building. Turn left and go straight ahead to pass a small hotel on the left and then bear right to reach a caravan park.

Follow the path through the caravan park to enter the woods of Culzean by going over a stile. Continue straight ahead until you reach a car park on the left. Take the path that leads off to the left to pass the aviary and continue until you reach Swan Lake. This lives up to the name with swans among its inhabitants, together with various species of duck and herons.

Turn right and walk along the side of the lake before entering thick woodland, following the track which meanders through the rhododendrons and along the top of the cliffs, to emerge into open parkland just beyond the private residence of Dolphin House.

The magnificent splendour of Culzean Castle now strikes you full on. Go ahead over the parkland in a diagonal direction, through a gate, to emerge at the Orange conservatory. Lack of funds have so far prevented the conservatory from being renovated.

Culzean Castle, where American president Dwight D. Eisenhower had a room

Go left up the steps to reach the castle and continue straight ahead to reach the entrance. Beyond the entrance is an indicator viewpoint, with a magnificent panorama of the Firth of Clyde mirrored superbly in the blue waters rushing against the rocky coastline.

When you leave the castle, follow the path signposted to the Park Centre, formerly the Home Farm, now accommodating an exhibition area – including videos which depict the history of Culzean – a restaurant, and a gift shop.

One can spend a whole day at Culzean, exploring the numerous paths and avenues. Follow the roadway now that leads to the former light railway between Alloway Junction and Turnberry. It was opened in 1906, and although closed in 1931, it was re-opened a year later, but for only 11 months. The Maidens and Dunure Railway, built mainly to serve Turnberry golf course, was never a success. Part of the route has now been converted into a walkway.

At the rail bridge descend the steps on the left to the old

track and turn left. Pass over two bridges and continue, to go under a third bridge. After approximately 300 yards the track becomes more overgrown, and where the track peters out go down to the left and over a stile. Turn right and go down the road to reach the old building passed earlier in the walk. Turn left and walk back to your car.

Walk 16
THE DUBH LOCH (BLACK LOCH) OF LOCHNAGAR
GRAMPIAN
8 miles

Despite its name, Lochnagar isn't a loch but a mountain, and a fine one at that. It overlooks the royal country of Balmoral in Aberdeenshire and was a great favourite of Queen Victoria. The hill is possibly best known today as the title of one of Scotland's best loved songs, 'Dark Lochnagar', the words of which were written by Lord Byron. A children's book, 'The Old Man of Lochnagar', was written by no less an author than the Prince of Wales and published a few years ago. It apparently had its origins in a story that the Prince made up for his younger brothers while staying at Balmoral during the Royal summer holidays.

Close to Lochnagar and the village of Ballatar lies Loch Muick, and at its head, clenched in a deep-set mountain corrie, lies our objective – the Dubh Loch, a place of wild craggy hillsides and a superb wilderness atmosphere. This is the haunt of golden eagle and red deer – and climbers, in both summer and winter. The backcloth of dark brooding cliffs plunges down from the heights of Broad Cairn, and the setting well justifies the Gaelic name of Black Loch. This loch is much smaller than Loch Muick and being at an elevation of close on 2,000 feet can be covered with ice until well into the summer. Don't be tempted onto the ice, though, as it breaks up into great ice floes which can be difficult to get off.

If you're really lucky, you may spot a golden eagle or peregrine falcon up here, and from September to late Octo-

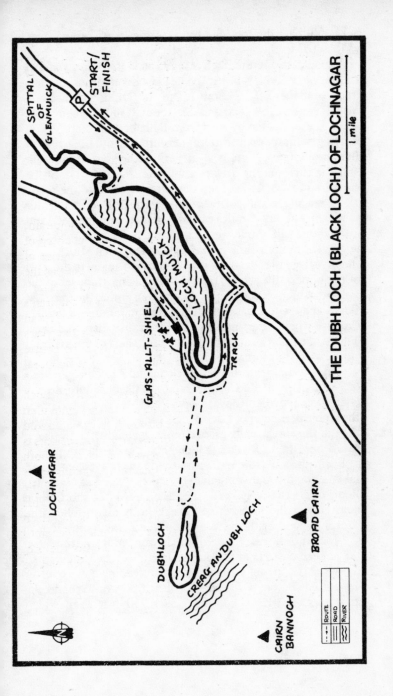

THE DUBH LOCH (BLACK LOCH) OF LOCHNAGAR

1 mile

SPITTAL OF GLENMUICK

START / FINISH

P

LOCH MUICK

GLAS-ALLT-SHIEL

TRACK

LOCHNAGAR

DUBH LOCH

CREAG AN DUBH LOCH

CAIRN BANNOCH

BROAD CAIRN

N

ROUTE
ROAD
RIVER

ber you'll hear the roaring of the rutting stags: a fine sound well suited to the mood of the place.

A good path circuits Loch Muick and it offers an attractive and easy low-level walk. At the head of Loch Muick another track branches off to climb up to the Dubh Loch. Loch Muick is a sizeable loch and lies about 1,300 feet above sea level. It's accessible by road from Ballater and offers a good starting point for many different excursions into these hills of Balmoral estate. There is a car park at the start of the walk and the surrounding area is a wildlife reserve, so don't be surprised to see herds of red deer grazing close to the road.

To reach the car park, cross the River Dee in Ballater (which lies about 40 miles east of Aberdeen, on the A93) and after about half a mile west on the south Deeside road turn left up the minor road which is signposted 'Glen Muick'. For the first five miles or so the road climbs gradually to the level of the upper valley floor, offering tantalising glimpses of the Falls of Muick on your right. After a short time, the tree-clad slopes change to a bare and featureless moorland, a treeless expanse which offers fine habitat for grouse, hare and deer. The road ends at a car park about a mile short of the loch and close by is an information hut.

Other walks from Glen Muick include Lochnagar itself (3,789 feet) and the Capel Mounth walk over into nearby Glen Doll and Glen Clova. Good Land Rover tracks circuit the whole perimeter of Loch Muick; once the deer are shot on the hill they are usually carried or dragged down to the track side where Land Rovers will come and pick them up.

From the car park walk past the interpretive centre and take the road which immediately strikes off across the valley floor, or alternatively keep straight on until just short of the near end of the loch where a track leads off to follow the shore. A good bridge crosses the river at this point.

From the shores of Loch Muick you can begin to realise the superb position of the place. On either side it is hemmed in by steep slopes of scree and heather, leading down over an abrupt edge from a virtual plateau which stops around the 2,000 feet mark. The loch is over 250 feet deep which

The Dubh Loch of Lochnagar, a remote and wild stretch of water amid the Royal land of Balmoral.

indicates perhaps that the valley was created by glaciation. As further proof of this theory the north end of the loch is dammed by glacial deposits now covered by deep peat.

Along either side of the loch are a few old birch trees, one of the species which used to flourish in these parts. Regeneration of the birch is now virtually impossible, simply due to the presence of red deer. Whenever the young shoots begin to show above the ground they're nibbled by hungry deer, so there is no chance of new growth.

On the north-west side of the loch, close to its southern end, stand the buildings of Glass Allt Shiel, a modest shooting lodge built on the instructions of Queen Victoria. The name of the lodge is taken from the tumbling burn which roars down from Lochnagar behind. If you have time, it's worthwhile taking a walk up by the burn to view the Glas Allt Falls, where the burn begins its plunge down from the plateau.

At the southern extremity of the loch one of the burns entering is the Allt an Dubh Loch, and on the north side of this stream an easy track leads upwards to the secluded Dubh Loch itself.

Return by the track to Loch Muick, but bear right, round the western end, so you can walk back to the car park by the shore opposite the one you followed earlier.

Walk 17
BENNACHIE IRON AGE FORT
GRAMPIAN
6 or 3 miles

Although little over 500 metres in height, Bennachie ranks
as one of the best-loved landmarks in Aberdeenshire, and one
of the best-known 'wee hills' in Scotland. Dominating the
farm plains of the area known as the Garioch (pronounced
Geeree), and the further low farmlands of Buchan, Bennachie is also a welcome landmark for fishermen returning to
Aberdeen and the Aberdeenshire fishing ports after extended
fishing trips to the North Sea. And indeed, many people who
have never seen the hill will be familiar with the Aberdeenshire song which runs:

Oh, gin I were where the Gadie rins,
Far Gadie rins, far Gadie rins,
Oh, gin I were far Gadie rins,
At the fit o'Bennachie.

Many will know the song as a pipe tune which was adopted
as the regimental march of the Gordon Highlanders. The
Gadie, by the way, is the stream on the north side of the hill.
Gazing at Bennachie from a distance, on the long ridge of
the hill its prominent tors at either end resemble breasts, and
some believe that the name of the hill is taken from this
feature, as in Beinn Chioch, or the hill of paps.
Bennachie, then, is a distinctive ridge, about three miles
long, with a series of distinctive tops. The highest of the tops
is the Oxen Craig (1,733ft) but the most interesting, and the
best-known is the slightly shorter easternmost point called

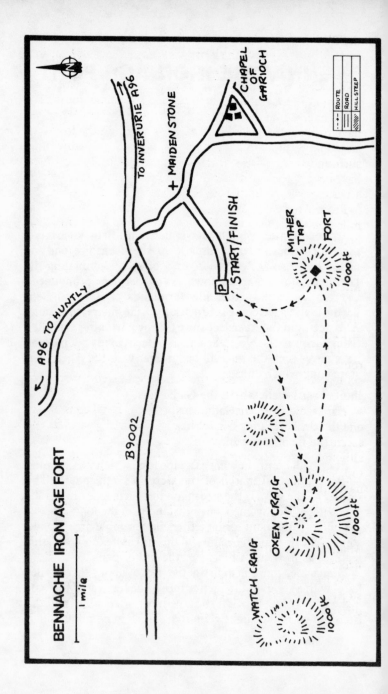

the Mither Tap. Up here, overlooking the rich farm lands and the blue waters of the North Sea, lies an ancient Iron Age fortress sitting on top of a great granite block.

We know very little about these Pictish people, or of how they built these hilltop forts, but the construction must have taken many man-hours and tremendous effort. What we have remaining on the Mither Tap is a 15 foot thick wall of large stones built in a circular shape which probably once surrounded the whole of the hill's summit. The fort must have been of some considerable size and was probably used as a place of refuge by the Picts of the surrounding areas.

From Aberdeen, take the main A96 road to about three miles beyond the town of Inverurie. Just before the A96 bends right, at the junction with the B9002, turn left onto a minor road which leads to Chapel of Garioch. But after about three-quarters of a mile from the A96, just beyond the Maiden Stone – an inscribed Pictish standing stone just to the left of the road – take the road to the left which is clearly signposted 'Bennachie Car Park' and follow it to the car park at the end.

There is a choice of walks from here to the fort: the direct route to Mither Tap, no more than three miles in total, or the six mile route which takes the walker via Oxen Craig. The shorter is described first.

The ascent from the car park to the Mither Tap is about one and a half miles and involves just over a thousand feet of ascent, none of it too steep. The track is good all the way, although it crosses over several estate roads en route to the top. These are all marked 'private' so they shouldn't pose any navigational problems.

The first part of the ascent is through the forest and is the steepest. After about half a mile though it eases off and you will find yourself on a very old track. This is the ancient Maiden's Causeway, which runs most of the length of Bennachie.

As the summit slopes are approached the track leaves the stony causeway and after crossing a small stream makes directly to the top. Within a hundred feet of the top you will

Bennachie, a well-known landmark in Aberdeenshire and site of an ancient fort.

pass through the entrance of the fort where you will see how the stones have been built up to create this very thick wall. The path picks its way up stones to the top, and there are many fine variants to choose, particularly if you fancy the idea of a simple rock scramble.

The view from the summit is quite extensive, overlooking Aberdeenshire, Garioch, Feughside, Deeside and even as far as the Cairngorms. An indicator, implemented by Mr James McKey, Depute Senior Baillie of Bennachie was erected a few years ago with the help of teachers and pupils from Inverurie Academy.

In 1973 a local group called the Baillies of Bennachie was formed to look after the hills in view of the greatly increased number of visitors in recent years.

The longer route to the hill fort follows a path, completed in 1973 by the Forestry Commission, leading south from the car park then west through the woods to the top of Oxen Craig. From there, take the path eastwards to Mither Tap – another route established by the Forestry Commission, and a welcome one, for this long whaleback ridge of Bennachie is covered all year in deep heather, arduous to walk through. The descent from Mither Tap follows the route taken by the shorter walk.

Walk 18
ARTHUR'S SEAT
LOTHIAN
4 miles

Edinburgh, Scotland's capital city, has been called the Athens of the north – a city of many gems, and the jewel in Scotland's crown. It is famous for its castle, the Palace of Holyrood, the Royal Mile, Princes Street, and the Calton Hill.

Yet, set in the middle of this city of almost half a million people are additional fine attractions for the walker: many acres of open parkland, such as Holyrood Park – a rich area of pastureland and green dominated by the volcanic rock of Arthur's Seat. It is on this ancient foundation that the city is built, and from many parts of the city as well as the high hills of the Borders and Fife the rock can be seen as the dominating feature of this festival city.

There is so much else for the visitor to see in Edinburgh that Arthur's Seat might easily be neglected. Yet the rock looms over Holyrood Palace, like some majestic guardian, defending the residence of the Queen while she is in the city. The parkland takes the explorer away from the continuous throbbing of traffic to a quiet country within a city.

The walk begins at Duddingston Loch, a bird sanctuary and nature reserve where there are varied interesting species of duck and geese. It adjoins Duddingston village, with its twelfth-century church. The area is well served by Lothian Regional Council public bus services and details of all local services are obtainable from their headquarters in the city's Queen Street.

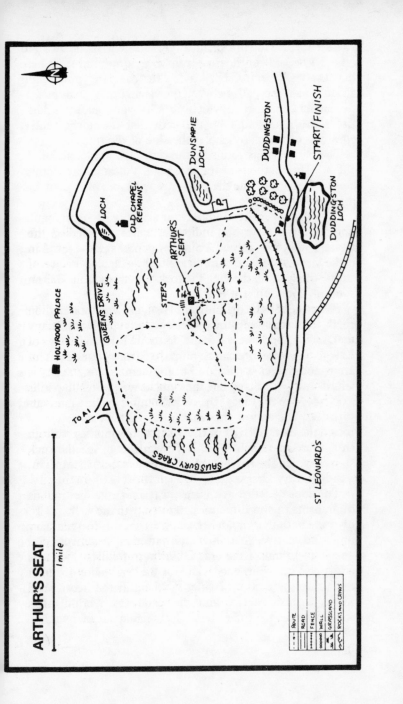

There is parking in a small lay-by at the end of the loch and on the other side of the road from the church; it is from here that the walk begins. On leaving the car park, go straight ahead up a steep path between gorse and other small bushes to reach a second road which plies its way round the park. Cross the road and take the path that meanders gently, climbing occasionally, along the side of the hill.

The path swings round to the right in a moderate curve, and you should then go straight ahead. Volcanic rock dominates to the right while the grass-strewn slopes offer contrasting monochromes to the left.

As you go over the crest, Arthur's Seat, with its triangulation point and viewpoint indicator, comes into view approximately 300 yards ahead. A number of paths criss-cross here; make straight for the summit, taking particular care on the paths which climb through the rocky outcrops to the 823 foot summit. Hold on if it is windy.

From the top the magnificent views are breathtaking. The Firth of Forth sweeps majestically down via North Berwick to Dunbar, and the Lomond Hills in Fife and even Ben Lawers in Perthshire can be pinpointed on a clear day. There are panoramic views of Edinburgh, seemingly only an arm's length away; for that alone the climb is well worth the effort.

Descend to the foot of the rocky summit by the same route, turn left, and follow the track in an easterly direction and round the eastern flank of the Seat, where another path rises from Dunsapie Loch. Go ahead down a set of specially made steps to reach the narrow valley which dissects Arthur's Seat and Salisbury Crags.

The tops of Salisbury Crags, a face of rock over 60 feet high, brings a new dimension of the city to the walker. Cross over the path that divides the crags from the Seat and climb onto the plateau to follow the path that leads round the curving summit of the crags. The path follows close to the edge, and there are good views of the remainder of the city including the castle, St Giles' Cathedral, the Scott Monument, Princes Street, and the famous Waverley railway station from where the Flying Scotsman made many notable excursions.

Arthur's Seat, with its panoramic views of Edinburgh

It is pleasant walking on the crags: gentle, rolling, and descending slowly. On the right, on the west face of the Seat, a narrow cleft of rock, not unlike a house chimney, tapers out into whin and scree, and finally grass. One can descend by this route, but it is not recommended.

Once again cross the path that runs through the valley, but do not go as far as the small lochan, over which stand the stone remains of an old chapel. Follow the path to the right, climbing easily between rocks to the foot of the Seat. Turn left onto the path and steps descended earlier in the walk.

Climb to the top of the steps and then take the path that doubles back and goes round in a horseshoe curve to reach the loch of Dunsapie. At the road turn right and pass a lay-by to where a fence begins on the left.

A number of steps leads down from here to grassland and then a large wall. Turn right and descend on the path to the road at Duddingston Loch, helped by a series of steps. Turn right to reach the car park just beyond a cottage.